ANCIENT CIVILIZATIONS

China

By Tami Deedrick

STECK-VAUGHN
ELEMENTARY · SECONDARY · ADULT · LIBRARY

A Harcourt Company

www.steck-vaughn.com

Library of Congress Cataloging-in-Publication Data is available upon request.

Printed and bound in the United States of America
10 9 8 7 6 5 4 3 2 1 W 04 03 02 01

Photo Acknowledgments
Corbis/Brian Vikander, 8; Pierre Colombel, 11; Archivo Iconografico, 14; Burstein Collection, 16, 24; Pierre Colombel, 18, 47; Bettmann, 31; Horace Bristol, 34
NASA, 37
Photo Network, 27, 38; Bachmann, 12
Root Resources/Claudia Adams, cover, 40; Shirley Hodge, title page
Visuals Unlimited, 28; Bill Kamin, 20, 32; Jeff Greenberg, 22; Robin Karpan, 42

Contents

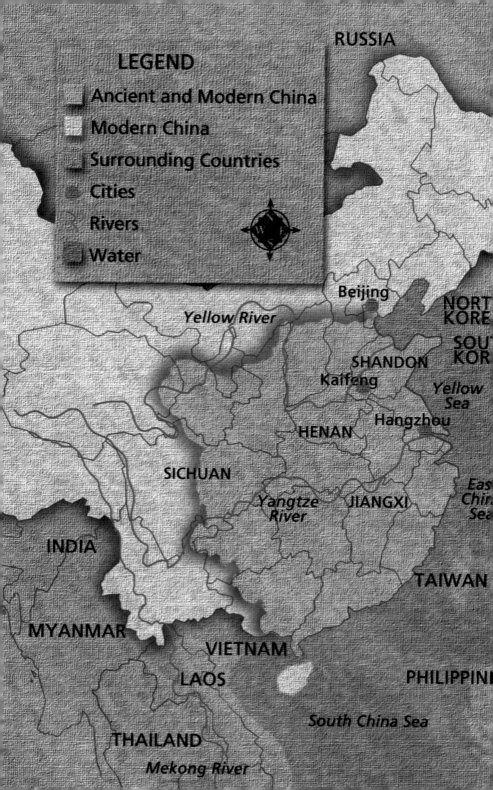

China has a long history. Over thousands of years, China has changed and grown. Chinese people formed a great **civilization**. A civilization is an advanced **society**. A society shares a common way of life.

The Chinese people have lived on the same land since the beginning of their history. China is the largest country in the Far East. The Far East is an area of eastern Asia that borders the north Pacific Ocean.

Chinese people did many great things. They started their own language and way of writing. They built large cities and palaces. They invented new things, such as fireworks.

Early Chinese History

China's history covers thousands of years. Many different dynasties ruled China. A **dynasty** is a family or group that rules or stays in power for several years.

The Qin (CHIN) dynasty (221 to 206 B.C.) brought the Chinese people together into one nation. To protect their land, the people united earlier walls to make one Great Wall in 214 B.C. The Great Wall ran from the sea to the desert along the mountains in northern China. The name "China" probably came from the Qin. The Qin dynasty ended when the people fought against their rulers.

The Han (HAHN) was the next dynasty. During this time, the Chinese took over new land and began making more silk. Silk is a cloth made from silkworm cocoons. The Chinese traded silk with many other people around the world. War ended the Han dynasty.

TIMELINE OF SELECTED CHINESE DYNASTIES

221 to 206 B.C.	Qin Dynasty
207 B.C. **to** A.D. **220**	Han Dynasty
589–618	Sui Dynasty
619-907	Tang Dynasty
960-1279	Song Dynasty
1279-1368	Yuan Dynasty
1368-1644	Ming Dynasty
1645-1910	Qing Dynasty
1911-1948	Republic of China
1949 to present	People's Republic of China

The Chinese people fought wars between themselves after the Han dynasty. Other dynasties came into power, but they did not last long.

This is a sculpture of a powerful king from a Chinese dynasty.

Later Chinese History

The Tang (TAHNG) dynasty brought China together again. People thought of new ideas in printing, farming, and poetry. But new wars between Chinese people ended the Tang dynasty, too.

Another time of unity began with the Song (SOONG) dynasty. When the Mongols attacked China and won, they began the Yuan (yoo-AHN) dynasty. After almost 100 years of foreign rule, the Chinese fought back and won. Foreign means coming from another country. The people established the Ming (MING) dynasty. The Manchu attacked the Ming. They started a new dynasty called the Qing (CHING) dynasty.

The Chinese people came together again to remove the Manchu. They formed a **republic**. A republic is a form of government where the people vote for rulers.

Some Chinese people did not like the republic. They fought their rulers and formed a communist government. **Communism** began during this period and continues today. Communism is a way of organizing a country so the government owns everything and the people share the wealth.

The Song (960-1279)

This book is about the three dynasties that lasted from A.D. 960 to 1644. These dynasties are the Song, the Yuan, and the Ming.

A group of soldiers named their leader, Zhao Kuangyin (JOW KWAHNG-YIN), the emperor in 960. Zhao rebuilt the government with people who were loyal to him.

Zhao named the dynasty Song after his childhood home. The capital was in the north at Kaifeng (kay-FUHNG). When Zhao died, his family ruled the dynasty.

In 1127, a group called the Jin (JIN) attacked Kaifeng. The royal family was captured, except for the ninth son of the emperor. Captured means caught and held by force. His name was Gaozong (GOW-DZOONG). Gaozong fled to the south. He established the Song capital in the southern city of Hangzhou (HAHNG-JOE).

This is a painting of an emperor who ruled during the Song dynasty.

The Great Wall is the only human-made object that can be seen from outer space without a telescope.

The Yuan (1279-1368)

The Chinese people in the north were still fighting the Mongols. The great warrior Genghis Khan led the Mongols as they swept across Asia. In 1215, the Mongols took over northern China. In 1279, the Mongol leader Kublai Khan finally took over the Song in southern China. He named his dynasty Yuan because it means beginning.

The Mongols set up their government in China and kept fighting. They allowed the Chinese people to rule in lower positions.

The Ming (1368-1644)

After time, the Chinese people rebelled against their Mongol rulers. A monk named Zhu Yuanzhang (JOO YWEN-JAHNG) led the army that chased the Mongols back to their land in the north. He called his dynasty Ming. The word Ming means bright and shining.

The Ming rebuilt the Great Wall. They also built the Forbidden City. The Forbidden City was a place where the emperors lived during the next two dynasties.

These Chinese people are spinning silk thread into cloth.

Daily Life in Ancient China

There were four main social classes in China. A class is a group of people that have similar jobs.

The highest class was made of the royal family. They ruled the people. The emperor was the most important person in China.

Below the royal family was the Shi (SHUR). The Shi were the nobles and scholars. The nobles were powerful, rich people.

The largest group of people was the Nong. The Nong were mostly poor farmers.

The Gong were the craftspeople. They made objects to sell, such as silk or dishes.

The Shang sold and traded the goods the craftspeople produced. This made them rich.

▲ **These Shi scholars are wearing robes tied with sashes.**

Clothing

Most Chinese people wore the same style of clothing. Men and women wore long robes tied with belts or sashes. Under their robes, women sometimes wore trousers that were tight at the ankle.

The farmers and craftspeople wore clothes made of hemp or cotton. Their robes were often shorter than the robes of the wealthy. Shorter robes helped them move around more easily while they worked. In the summer, they wore one layer of clothing to keep cool. In the winter, they wore many layers to keep warm.

The wealthy wore silk robes. They wore light silk in the summer and heavier silk called satin in the winter. Sometimes the silk was dyed different colors or painted with designs.

Men wore tall, rounded hats with long strings called feet. A piece of wire or bamboo made the feet bendable. Powerful men in government often wore their feet straight. Less powerful men wore the feet curved or crossed. Sometimes the high officials wore lifts on their shoes. Lifts were little platforms that made the men look taller.

Women braided and twisted their hair into high buns on top of their heads. They decorated the buns with pins and combs.

This is the ceiling from a palace where the emperor lived.

Homes

Many wealthy Chinese people had large brick houses with many rooms and levels. The houses were often built around two courtyards. A courtyard is an open place surrounded by walls or buildings. The courtyards held beautiful gardens, fruit trees, and small ponds. Colorful yellow or green tiles covered the roofs. Fences often surrounded the houses.

Feather beds, silk couches, and wooden tables stood inside the homes of the wealthy. They also had their own private bathrooms. Gold and jewels decorated the rooms. Silk hung from the walls. The wealthy almost always had flowers in every room.

The common people built houses that were much smaller and less decorated. In some places, they built with mud bricks and stone. In other places, they used bamboo and wood to build the walls. Leaves and reeds made the thatched roof. Houses usually had only one big room and no bathroom. The people used public bathrooms outside on the streets.

People slept on bamboo mats that could be rolled up and put away. They did not have much furniture. Some poor people decorated their homes with small clay statues.

Modern Chinese still grow rice in paddies as the ancient Chinese did.

Food

Rice and wheat were the main food of the Chinese people. Southern Chinese people grew rice in flooded fields called paddies. The Ming added fish to their rice paddies. The fish helped make the soil in the paddies rich. People also ate the fish.

The Chinese people boiled, steamed, and fried rice. They ground it into flour and used it to make bread. Sometimes they seasoned the rice with garlic, sesame, and ginger. Women often cooked vegetables in a **wok**. A wok is a frying pan shaped like a bowl. The Chinese also ate pork and other meats from rabbits, geese, and ducks.

The Yuan and the Ming dynasties added other items to the Chinese diet. The Yuan included milk and tea. The Ming added peanuts, sweet potatoes, corn, and sugar cane. The Ming also planted millions of fruit trees.

The Chinese served food in **pottery** bowls or porcelain dishes. They ate with **chopsticks**. Chopsticks are thin sticks used to pick up food.

This clay statue was made during the Song dynasty.

Ancient Chinese Culture

A group of people's ideas, customs, traditions, and way of life make up their **culture**. Chinese people expressed their culture through the things they did and the things they made. The Chinese culture taught that people should act with honor. The Chinese respected their parents and elders.

Different dynasties developed different parts of Chinese culture. The Song culture focused on the arts. The Ming culture focused on knowledge. They wrote many books and studied many past Chinese dynasties. After being ruled by the foreign Manchu, they wanted to focus on all things Chinese.

▲ **This ancient Chinese artwork combines both calligraphy and painting.**

Art

The Chinese made great advances in calligraphy. Calligraphy is a form of beautiful Chinese writing using a brush to make a series of strokes called a word or character. The Chinese often combined their writing with paintings and poetry. Calligraphy was hard to learn. There are more than 10,000 characters or words in the written Chinese language.

Painting was another important art. Even the emperors studied painting. A Song emperor named Zhezong formed an early painting school. The Chinese painted mostly landscapes with mountains, streams, and gardens. They believed people and buildings were not as important as nature. Artists often painted in different shades of only one color.

Chinese people invented porcelain. Porcelain is made from white clay. The clay turns into light pottery that is almost like glass. That is one reason why porcelain dishes are called "china."

The porcelain made during the Ming dynasty became the most famous. Ming blue-and-white china is known throughout the world. Artists painted pictures on the white clay with a bright blue dye. Then they baked the clay until it hardened.

Architecture

Architecture is a style and way of building. The Chinese had a style of building that was easy to spot.

For many years, they built **pagodas** as parts of **temples**. A pagoda is a tall building with special roofs. The roofs looked ruffled and had pointed edges. A temple is a special building used for worshiping gods. Other buildings were built with the same pagoda style, but were not used as temples.

The Forbidden City

The Forbidden City was a palace built for the royal family during the Ming dynasty. The palace has more than 9000 rooms. It took 14 years to build, but it became home to 24 emperors during the next 500 years.

The Chinese built the city in the shape of a rectangle. It had a yellow roof and purple walls. They put a high wall and a **moat** all the way around it. A moat is a deep ditch filled with water. The Chinese called their moat the protective river.

Roofs in the Forbidden City were yellow. Yellow was a special color only the emperor could use.

The Forbidden City is now called the Gugong Museum in China. It is open for the public to tour. The museum displays more than one million rare items.

Modern Chinese still use the Grand Canal to move things around China.

The Grand Canal

The Grand Canal was another building achievement. A canal is a waterway built by people. The Grand Canal was originally built during the Sui dynasty (589–618). It connected three major rivers. It was used to carry goods on water from city to city.

Workers made the canal larger during the Yuan dynasty to link Beijing and Hangzhou. Chinese people kept making the canal larger. Over time, the canal grew to more than 1,000 miles (1,609 km) long. It linked northern and southern China.

Music and Literature

The Chinese people enjoyed theater. Plays were about people. Only a few written plays have lasted through the years. One collection called Yuanquxuan is still used today. Opera was a Chinese favorite. Opera is a play where all the words are sung instead of spoken.

The Chinese wrote many books. Novels first appeared in the Yuan dynasty. The Chinese wrote books about many things. There were histories, poetry, stories, and reference books. A reference is a book people use to find information easily. The Chinese also wrote religious books and books that explained the classic books.

School, Learning, and Writing

In early China, there were few schools. Parents taught their children at home. Mothers taught their children to read and say poems by memory.

In 1020, the government set up schools. They wanted at least one school in every area. The government provided the books and the land for the school. Boys went to the government-run schools. Girls stayed home and learned how to run a household.

After government schooling was finished, some students attended the National University in Kaifeng. There they studied the Chinese language and the classic books. They practiced calligraphy and learned new characters. Later, they were taught to write poems. The top students could take an exam called the jinshi. If they passed, this exam helped them get a job in the government.

> **This is an ancient Chinese abacus. Students used it to solve math problems.**

Chinese students used an **abacus** to count. An abacus has a square frame with wires that run from one side to the other. Round beads for counting are on the wires. The students moved the beads to do math problems.

The Chinese used advanced building methods to make this Bamboo Shoot Pagoda.

What Did the Chinese Do?

The Chinese people were always trying to fix everyday problems. Their inventions and discoveries happened because they were looking to make something better.

The Chinese were far ahead of the rest of the world in building methods. The Chinese discovered how to make bricks. People in other places cut stones to make buildings.

The Chinese also started the use of paper money. Most countries used coins. But paper was lighter and easier to handle than coins. The Song first started using paper money, but it became common in the Yuan dynasty.

Modern Chinese junks have the same design as ancient junks.

Sea Travel

The Chinese were excellent shipbuilders. They built large, flat-bottomed ships called **junks**. Each junk had watertight sections all along the bottom of the ship. If a section started leaking, the water would only flood that section and the ship would still float.

Junks also had moveable and removable **sails**. A sail is a large piece of cloth that catches the wind and pushes the ship. The Chinese could move the sail so the wind pushed the ship in the direction they wanted to travel.

The Chinese also developed locks on canals. Locks have gates on each end of a closed area that holds water inside. When a ship enters the lock, the gate at the open end is closed. The area then fills with water or lets the water flow out. The ship raises or lowers so it can go out the other end of the lock and into a new canal.

The Chinese also invented the compass. A compass is a tool used for finding directions. The Chinese used the compass to find their way in bad weather. The Chinese compass always points south.

Healing

The Chinese were also looking for ways to heal and help people. Scientists wanted to make the elixir of life. An elixir is a magic drink that makes people live forever. They believed the elixir of life would cure all sicknesses so people would not die. Many medicines came from the search for the elixir of life.

Acupuncture was invented in China. The Chinese put thin, sharp needles into special parts of the body. The Chinese believed the energy of life flowed along paths in the body. They thought they could move the energy by pressing needles along the path. Needles in different parts of the body were supposed to cure different sicknesses.

Astronomy

The Chinese studied the sky. They made maps of the stars and named them. They kept records of comets. A comet is a large ball of ice, dust, and rock that has a tail of

The Chinese studied the sky and kept track of comets like this one.

glowing gases when it is near the Sun. They also kept track of eclipses. An eclipse happens when the light of the Sun or the Moon is blocked for awhile.

Chinese scientists studied the sky to tell time and make calendars. The Chinese knew that there were more than 365 days in one year.

Archaeologists study building remains like the ruins of this Chinese palace.

How We Know

Chinese history has been kept well, starting with writings from thousands of years ago. Paintings and **artifacts** from the past tell stories about the Chinese and how they lived. An artifact is an object made or used by humans in the past.

Archaeologists search for artifacts. Archaeologists are scientists who study ancient, or old, remains. They study Chinese **tombs** and the things inside them. They also study the remains of ancient buildings. These things give archaeologists clues about what life was like for people in ancient China.

Clay soldiers, horses, carts, and weapons were buried near one emperor's tomb.

Writings

The Han dynasty was the first to write a history of China. They gathered information from old books, carved plates, jars, and stones. Then they wrote down what they discovered. All the dynasties after them also wrote down history.

Very few of the writings are still in their original form. They have been copied over the centuries. Scientists try to decide what is original and what might have been added when the writing was copied.

Emperor's Tomb

Archaeologists found one important site in 1974. The first emperor of the Qin dynasty, Shi Huangdi, died in 210 B.C. Before he died, he built a huge tomb. Ancient Chinese writers had described the tomb as filled with gold and silver. They told about 70,000 artists working on the tomb to make it beautiful. An army of clay soldiers, horses, and chariots were buried outside the tomb.

This walkway is part of the Ming Tombs.
Many people visit the Ming Tombs each year.

Ming Tombs

The Ming Tombs are the burial places of
13 of the 16 emperors of the Ming dynasty.
The Tombs are built in a large horseshoe
pattern. Ming emperors believed in an
afterlife. They built the tombs and filled

them with riches and everyday items they thought they would need. The Sacred Way leads to the Tombs. Large statues of Chinese officials and animals line the Sacred Way.

The Ming Tombs are about 25 miles (40 km) north of Beijing. The Chinese opened the Tombs to visitors in 1958.

China and the Modern World

Today, China is the third largest country in the world. More people live in China than anywhere else in the world. The people in China almost all have a Chinese background. Of the 8% that do not, some are Mongols, Manchus, and Koreans.

The Chinese culture changed when communism became the form of government. Art became focused on telling stories that the government thought would be helpful.

Many Chinese people now live in all parts of the world. No matter where the Chinese are, they create works that show the long and rich culture they have.

Glossary

abacus (AB-uh-kuhss)—a frame with sliding beads on wires that is used for counting

archaeologist (ar-kee-OL-uh-jist)—a scientist who studies ancient remains

artifact (ART-uh-fakt)—an object that was made or used by humans in the past

chopsticks (CHOP-stiks)—thin sticks used to pick up food

civilization (siv-i-luh-ZAY-shuhn)—a highly developed and organized society

communism (KOM-yuh-niz-uhm)—a way of ruling a country so the government owns everything and the people share the wealth

culture (KUHL-chur)—the way of life, ideas, customs, and traditions of a group of people

dynasty (DYE-nuh-stee)—a period of time in a country's history when one family ruled the nation

junk (JUHNGK)—a large, flat-bottomed ship

moat (MOHT)—a deep trench filled with water

pagoda (puh-GOH-duh)—a tall building with special roofs; the roofs look ruffled and have pointed edges.

pottery (POT-ur-ee)—objects made of baked clay

republic (ri-PUHB-lik)—a form of government where people choose their rulers by voting

sail (SAYL)—a large piece of cloth that catches the wind and pushes a ship

society (suh-SYE-uh-tee)—a group of people with a common way of life

temple (TEM-puhl)—a special building used for worshiping gods

tomb (TOOM)—a grave, room, or building used for holding a dead body and burial objects

wok (WAHK)—a frying pan shaped like a bowl

Internet Sites

Ancient China Daily Life
http://members.aol.com/Donnclass/Chinalife.
  html

China on Your Mind
http://www.chinaonyourmind.com/chinatravel
  /learnhp.html

Electronic Passport to Chinese History
http://www.mrdowling.com/613chinesehistory
  .html

Forbidden City: A Virtual Tour
http://www.chinavista.com/beijing/gugong/!st
  art.html

Minnesota State University e-Museum—China
http://www.anthro.mankato.msus.edu/
  prehistory/china/index.shtml

Useful Addresses

Chinese Embassy
Education Affairs
2712 Porter Street NW
Washington, DC 20008

Council for Cultural Affairs
102 Ai-Kuo East Road
Taipei, 100
Taiwan, Republic of China

▼ **These clay statues are of a Chinese family during the Song dynasty.**

Index